Disappearing GRASSLANDS

BY KEVIN J. COOK

ENVIRONMENT ALERT!

Gareth Stevens Publishing
MILWAUKEE

For a free color catalog describing Gareth Stevens's list of high-quality books, call 1-800-341-3569 (USA) or 1-800-461-9120 (Canada).

ISBN 0-8368-0483-X

A Gareth Stevens Publishing edition

Edited and designed by The Creative Spark of
San Clemente, California, for
Gareth Stevens Publishing
1555 North RiverCenter Drive, Suite 201
Milwaukee, Wisconsin 53212, USA

Picture Credits
Nate Bacon, © 1993, pp. 18, 19; F.J. Baker/Dembinsky Photo Assoc, © 1993, pp. 2-3; Mike Barlow/Dembinsky Photo Assoc, © 1993, pp. 8 (upper), 9; William Bertschy, pp.8 (middle), 11 (lower); Willard Clay/ Dembinsky Photo Assoc, © 1992, front & back cover; pp.7, © 1992 pp.16-17; Sharon Cummings/Dembinsky Photo Assoc, © 1993, p. 6; Howard Garrett/Dembinsky photo Assoc, © 1993, pp. 20-21; James C. Godwin, © 1989, p. 23; Stephen Graham/Dembinsky Photo Assoc, © 1993, p. 14; Thomas R. Jones, pp. 4-5, 24 (upper); Alan G. Nelson/Dembinsky Photo Assoc, © 1993. p. 13; Ted Nelson/Dembinsky Photo Assoc, © 1992, p. 10; Stan Osolinski/ Dembinsky Photo Assoc, © 1993; front cover (inset), pp.10-11, 12 (upper), © 1991 p. 27; Beth Painter, p. 20; Jonathan Perry, p. 25 (right); Carl R. Sams, II/Dembinsky Photo Assoc, © 1993, p. 12 (lower); Wendy Shattil/Bob Rozinski, © 1991, p. 11 (upper), ©1988, p.15, p.24, © 1993, p.25 (left); Brian Vikander ©, p. 8 (lower).

Project editor: Patricia Lantier-Sampon
Series design: Laurie Shock
Book design: Elayne Roberts
Editorial coordinator and photo research: Elayne Roberts
Editorial consultant: Gregory Lee
Art direction: Elayne Roberts
Illustrations: Teri Rider

Printed in the United States of America
1 2 3 4 5 6 7 8 9 98 97 96 95 94 93

At this time, Gareth Stevens, Inc., does not use 100 percent recycled paper, although the paper used in our books does contain about 30 percent recycled fiber. This decision was made after a careful study of current recycling procedures revealed their dubious environmental benefits. We will continue to explore recycling options.

Production Director

President

CONTENTS

Words that appear in the glossary are printed in **boldface** type the first time they appear in the text.

THE SEA OF GRASS

If you stand on a hill, you can look across the **prairie** and watch the wind blow through the grass. Many people think the prairie looks like the ocean. The hills, and the low places between them, remind people of the way the ocean's water swells up and down. The wind makes the grass ripple just like small waves on the ocean's surface. The prairie is like a sea of grass.

Grasses make grasslands in the same way that trees make forests. Some grasses grow beneath forest trees, but grasslands are those places where grasses are the most abundant kind of plant. Before they began to disappear, grasslands covered large areas of land, some as large as small seas.

Grasslands occur on every continent except Antarctica. Plants bow before the wind as it moves across the land. This movement reminds many people of waves upon the ocean and leads them to call the grasslands "seas of grass."

4

Life Among the Grasses

Grasses make up the third largest family of plants in the world. Only the orchid and sunflower families have more species. We get many important foods from the grass family. Corn, wheat, oats, rice, barley, sugar cane, and bamboo are all different kinds of grasses.

Perennials are the most important kinds of grasses for forming grasslands. They have either special roots or underground stems called **rhizomes** that can survive dry years and cold seasons. Unlike perennial grasses that live for many years, **annuals** must grow from seeds every year. They grow quickly when soil is left bare, such as after a fire or after being trampled by grazing animals. Some grasses spread by forming **tillers**, which are new plants that grow from the base of the stem or from rhizomes.

Above: Wheat grass is the most widely grown crop plant in the world. Humans have grown wheat for thousands of years. It grows well where native prairies once covered the land.

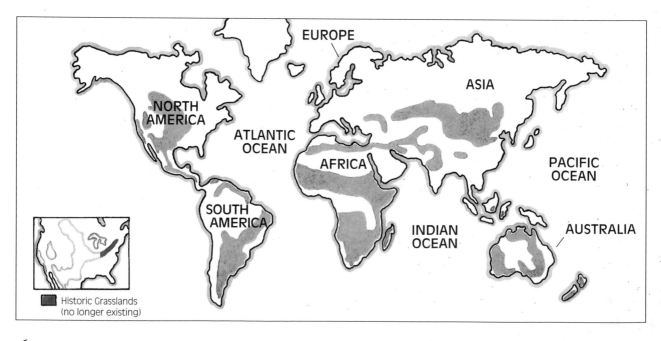

EUROPE

ASIA

NORTH
AMERICA

ATLANTIC
OCEAN

AFRICA

PACIFIC
OCEAN

SOUTH
AMERICA

INDIAN
OCEAN

AUSTRALIA

Historic Grasslands
(no longer existing)

Above: More than grasses grow on the grasslands. The flowers of many forbs, such as these bluebonnets in the pea family, add color to the sea of grass.

Opposite, bottom: Grasslands cover parts of some islands plus areas of every continent except Antarctica. Grasslands occur wherever rainfall and moisture in the soil favor the growing of grasses instead of trees. The world's grasslands are much smaller now than they used to be. A narrow band of prairie once ran from the Great Plains in North America through the Great Lakes region almost to the Atlantic Ocean (inset), but most of that area has been changed to farmland or forest.

Because of their thin shape, grasses can grow very close together. In some grasslands, grass plants grow so close together that you cannot see the soil beneath them.

Although grasses make the grasslands, the grasslands are more than just grasses. **Forbs** are the plants most people think of as wildflowers. With wide leaves and showy flowers, they do not look like grasses. Cattails, sedges, and rushes grow mostly in wet areas of the grasslands. They look like grasses, but each of them belongs to its own plant family. You can easily recognize grasses by their long, narrow leaves and by their flowers all bunched at the tip of slender, round stems.

Grasslands of the World

Water and fire are two natural elements that help form grasslands. The water comes from either rain or snow, sometimes both. Most grasslands get less than 40 inches (102 centimeters) of **precipitation** each year. How well the soil holds water can be more important to grasses and trees than how much precipitation falls. If the soil is too dry, trees die soon after they sprout from their seeds. Their leaves lose water faster than their roots can absorb it. Grasses can survive in dry soil better than trees because grasses grow the right kind of roots very quickly.

Above: The grasses and other plants of the western Great Plains in North America grow very short. This makes for a very simple grassland beauty.

Below: The Australian grasslands are home to many unique animals that have no related species anywhere else in the world.

The soil of some grasslands holds enough water for trees to grow. The grasslands survive because natural fires caused by lightning kill the trees. The seeds, roots, and rhizomes of grasses survive in the soil. Grasses often grow back very quickly when rain follows a fire.

Above: The most famous grassland in the world is the savanna of Africa. Here, tall acacia trees dot the sea of grass. A great many kinds of animals live here, and this diversity makes the savanna special.

Opposite, bottom: Bactrian camels live on the steppe of Asia. As people have changed the steppe for grazing and farming, the bactrian camel has disappeared. It now survives only in small desert grasslands of Mongolia and China.

The world has many different kinds of grasslands. A "savanna" is a grassland where trees grow scattered about. In South America, grasslands that are flooded for part of the year are called "llanos." Every continent has huge areas where only grasses and forbs grow. People call it the "prairie" in North America, the "pampas" in South America, the "veld" in South Africa, and the "steppe" in Europe and Asia. People often confuse **plains** for prairie. The confusion probably happens because the prairie grows on the American Great Plains. Not all plains are covered by prairie or other grassland types.

9

Animals of the Grasslands

Grasslands first began to appear on the planet Earth about 20 million years ago. Animals quickly learned to use the grasslands, and, today, they use the sea of grass the same as other animals use the ocean. Some animals live on or above the surface, and some animals live beneath the surface.

Each grassland region of the world has its own kind of animals. The plant-eating animals are called **herbivores**. Some prefer to **graze** on grasses and forbs, but others **browse** on woody plants. **Bison**, pronghorns, and elk are important grazers in North America. Llamas graze the South American pampas. Zebras and antelopes live on the African grasslands. Horses, camels, and antelopes roam the Asian steppe. Kangaroos wander the Australian grasslands.

Grasslands can survive the eating habits of the large grazing animals that evolved with them. Zebras (1) of the African savanna, bison (2) and pronghorns (3) of the American prairie, and llamas (4) of the Argentine pampas could cause severe problems if moved to other grasslands around the world.

Many kinds of birds also live on the grassland surface. Hawks, pipits, and sparrows are common grassland birds. Songbirds like to get above the ground so their songs can be heard better, but grasslands have few trees or shrubs the birds can perch on for singing. Grassland songbirds **skylark** to make themselves heard. They fly up into the air, then sing while gliding back to the ground!

Each large grassland area of the world has special birds that perform loud calls and dances. In North America, male prairie-chickens gather on areas called **leks** to dance and call. Females are attracted to the leks by the males.

Above: Bustards are a large family of mostly grassland birds. Africa and Asia have the most species, but a few kinds live in Europe and Australia. Many species have suffered as their grassland habitat has been lost. This is a black-bellied bustard from Africa.

The Black-footed Ferret

A member of the weasel family, the black-footed ferret once lived over most of the North American prairie. The ferret almost became extinct because people destroyed so much of its habitat. A few animals were found and trapped alive in the early 1980s. Almost 400 ferrets are now kept in captivity. One day, many will be turned loose to live in the wild grasslands of Wyoming.

Above, right: Meercats belong to the mongoose family. They live in burrows they dig in grassland soil. Meercats are important in a very complex food web involving many plants, insects, reptiles, birds, and mammals.

Opposite, bottom: A familiar grassland bird, the burrowing owl lives in abandoned rodent burrows. Though common in prairie dog towns of North America, they also live in the grasslands of Central and South America plus some islands of the West Indies.

Africa and Asia have no prairie-chickens, but they do have bustards. In India, the male lesser florican, a kind of bustard, claims a territory then leaps and leaps! He must jump 10 feet (3 meters) into the air so females can find him in the tall grass. South America has neither prairie-chickens nor bustards. Tinamous live in the grasslands there.

Fossorial animals live in the soil beneath the prairie. Examples of fossorial animals include aardvarks and meercats in Africa; and box turtles, badgers, and black-tailed prairie dogs on the American prairie. Burrowing owls often live in burrows that prairie dogs no longer use. All these animals can survive cold winters, dry summers, and even fires by staying in their burrows.

The Tide of Loss

All the great grasslands of the world are disappearing, and people are the cause. Human activities such as farming and ranching are two reasons the grasslands are being destroyed.

Grassland soils are so fertile they make the best farmlands in the world. Plowing and planting crops, however, destroy the grassland environment. Farmers sometimes pump too much water from the ground to **irrigate** crops. This causes wet areas of the grasslands to go dry. Many grassland animals need pools or other wet areas to survive. Ranching can also be harmful. All over the world, people have put too many cattle and sheep on grasslands. The animals eat too much and destroy the grasses.

Below: Everyone needs the food and clothing that farming and ranching provide, but poor farming and ranching practices have destroyed much of the world's grasslands. Better ways of growing crops and livestock could allow some grasslands to recover.

Above: Grassland habitat gets smaller as cities on the grasslands get bigger. These mule deer live on prairie outside Denver, Colorado. Many cities now protect small patches of prairie as parks or open space, but small patches cannot preserve the full beauty of the sea of grass.

Other causes of grassland destruction include building cities, putting out fires, and planting trees. As people make their cities and towns bigger, some of the natural environment is lost. Every building, parking lot, and highway takes up space. When that space is part of the grasslands, then building adds to grassland destruction. When people put out grassland fires, they save their own property; but without fire, trees can slowly take over and ruin the grasslands. A few trees grow naturally on grasslands, but Americans plant almost 20 million more trees on the prairie each year, believing trees are more important than grass. Unfortunately, this destroys more grasslands.

FACT FILE
The Most Endangered Land in America

The United States has more than 350 different sites in its National Park Service system. Many mountains, canyons, seashores, forests, rivers, and even buildings are protected as national parks or monuments. Not one park has ever been created to protect grasslands. We have a national Forest Service to take care of our forests and woodlands. Many states also have state forest agencies. We have no prairie or grassland service. The Forest Service cares for places called national grasslands, but these are used mostly for grazing cattle.

Many national groups have been formed to save special plants, animals, and wild lands, but no one has formed a national group to save the prairie. Many plants and animals have disappeared from the American grasslands, and others have become very rare. Because people changed the grasslands so much before scientists began to study them, no one is sure how much has been lost. One point is certain. No truly natural grasslands survive in North America.

In 1937, the U.S. Congress passed a special law. This law allowed the government to buy the farmland destroyed by the great drought of the 1930s from bankrupt farmers. Most of those lands, such as the Little Missouri National Grassland, became part of the national grassland system.

THE EFFORT TO SAVE THE GRASSLANDS

Scientists who study the grasslands know how important they are. Men and women in science today are working to find ways to protect the grasslands. People will always need to farm and to raise livestock, but new ideas can help these people and also help the grasslands.

Improving Our Farms

Scientists have learned how to breed special kinds of plants that are resistant to diseases and are not so easily eaten by insects. They also study better ways to grow crops. When farmers use special plants and better ways of growing, the farmland produces more food. This means less land has to be farmed.

Special programs also help farmers leave part of their land in its natural habitat. This means they do nothing to change it. These natural areas allow grassland plants and animals to survive. One law protects some prairie from **sodbusting**, or farming it for the first time.

Above: Every year, farmers plow up grassland soils to make old farms bigger or to make new farms.

Opposite: Practices such as plowing side-to-side across hills help preserve soil so farms last longer. Also, leaving woodland and forest patches between farms provides habitat for plants and animals that need trees. The same practice could mix native, unplowed grassland with farms so that more grassland plants and animals can survive.

Changing Our Ranches

Ranches raise animals instead of plants. Cattle, goats, and sheep are the most common ranch animals. Because these animals are so big and need so much food, ranches usually cover very large areas. Grasslands have always been important for ranching, but not everyone agrees on how ranching affects the grasslands. Some scientists believe grasslands need large grazing animals to eat the grasses.
They claim that cattle and sheep replace the feeding habits of native animals, like buffalo, that have disappeared. Other scientists believe cattle and sheep grazing is bad for grasslands.

Above: Livestock grazing on the left side of this fence keeps plants snipped low, which offers less habitat for grassland wildlife. Elk grazing on the right side of the fence leave taller plants and a greater variety. This shows how different species of grazing animals can either improve or damage a grassland.

Above: Cattle grazing, if managed well, doesn't have to be harmful to grasslands. If ranchers don't graze too many cattle for too long, the grasslands can survive.

Some grasslands have always had large animals that eat the grasses. Some grasslands have had no natural herbivores larger than insects and rodents. These grasslands cannot be grazed heavily without damage. Not all grazers eat the same parts of the grass plants, and different animals eat at different times of the year. Most large grazers **migrate**, or move from place to place. Many months or even years may pass before they graze the same grass again.

Below: Grass plants grow from the base up. This way of growing allows them to survive being eaten. Cattle usually eat the tops of the grasses, leaving enough plant to sprout new leaves. Sheep often snip the grass off right at the ground, making it hard for the plant to grow back. Africa has many large grazing animals. They migrate across the grasslands at different times. The first animals eat the top of the grass, the next animals eat the middle, and the last animals eat the bottom.

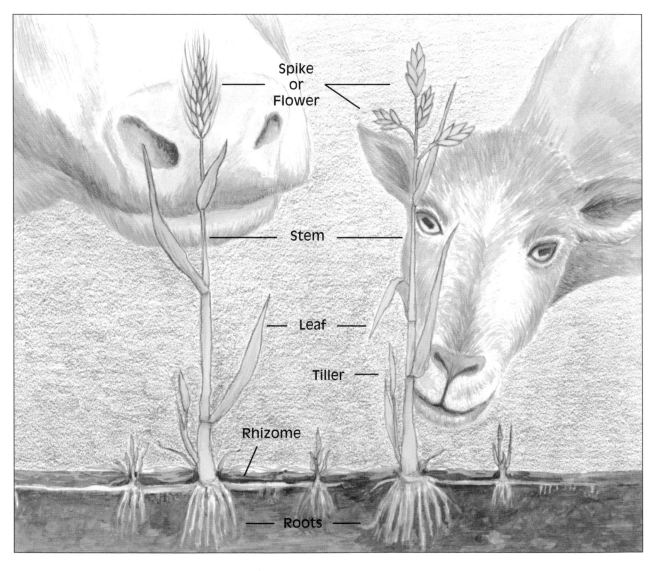

Spike or Flower

Stem

Leaf

Tiller

Rhizome

Roots

Above: Because sheep are smaller than cattle, more sheep than cattle can graze a grassland area. Sheep eat plants in a different way than cattle do. They also have smaller, sharper hooves. More sheep usually means more damage to grasslands.

Scientists and ranchers have studied how to control ranching so it does not ruin grasslands. Limiting how long and how many ranch animals graze on a grassland is very important. Removing ranch animals for a few months each year lets the grasslands rest just as they do when wild animals migrate. Different kinds of ranch animals can sometimes help protect a grassland, too. For example, browsers can help prevent woody plants from taking over the grasses.

Using Water More Carefully

Many grasslands are too dry for farming. If farms are built on dry grasslands, irrigating from wells or rivers can help the crops. It can also hurt the grasslands. Scientists are helping farmers select different crops that do not need so much water. They are also learning new ways of irrigating so that less water is used. Lining ditches with concrete, watering crops at certain times of day, and protecting the soil are good ways to save water. Saving water helps grasslands in two ways. First, it means more water for the grassland plants and animals. Second, it means less land is needed for farming.

Spadefoots

Spadefoots belong to their own special toad family. You can tell the difference between a spadefoot and a regular toad by the catlike pupil of its eye. The plains spadefoot can **estivate** when the prairie gets too dry. It may stay hidden in the soil for two years. After a heavy rain, it quickly becomes active again.

Above: Different kinds of farm crops need different amounts of water. By carefully choosing crops and matching them with the right method of irrigation, farmers save water.

Open Spaces

A few cities and towns are trying to protect small patches of grasslands. One way is to control where people build their houses and other buildings. Another way is to make natural grasslands part of city parks. Such places are often referred to as "open spaces" or natural areas. Special laws keep people from planting trees in these grassland parks.

Above: Central-pivot sprinklers pump water from the ground as they slowly move around a field to spray water over crops. New kinds of central-pivot systems use less water to irrigate crops better.

FACT FILE
Bringing Back the Fire

Many animals and people are afraid of fire. Fire can be very dangerous, but it can also be very useful. It heats our homes and cooks our food. It can also help people take care of grasslands.

Scientists have learned two important things about fire. First, it kills trees, shrubs, and forbs that can slowly take over grasslands. Second, it helps the soil. Plants take nutrients from the soil to build their roots, stems, leaves, flowers, and fruits. Some animals get their nutrients by eating the plants, but not all plants get eaten. As plants die, their parts must be broken down so the nutrients can be returned to the soil. Fire breaks down the dead plants by burning them. This helps put nutrients back in the soil for other plants to use.

Long ago, ancient people set fires to keep the land free of trees. In modern times, people have come to believe that fire is bad, so they try to put out all fires. People did not invent fire. It is as natural as rain and sunshine. Today, fires are sometimes set on purpose to keep grasslands healthy.

Above: Plants use nutrients in the soil to build their stems and leaves.
1. Nutrients from the soil become trapped in dead plant leaves.
2. Fire burns the dead plant leaves, which frees the nutrients.
3. Rain helps carry the nutrients back into the soil.
4. The same grasses can grow again using the nutrients freed by the fire.

Right: Some flowering plants begin to emerge from the path of a fire. Not all fire is bad. Fire is a natural process that many plants and animals need in order to survive. Sometimes, people carefully set fires on purpose just to keep grasslands healthy.

RESEARCH ACTIVITIES

1. **Learn how plants grow.**
   Get a color marker with ink that will not wash off. Go out into your yard. Make a short line across the width of a tree trunk, a flower stem, and a blade of grass. Check the marked plants each day for two weeks. Use a ruler to check how far above the ground the mark is on each plant. Which marks move? Which marks stay in the same place? What does this tell you about how the plants grow? What would happen to the flowers if you mowed them the same as you mow the grass?

2. **Compare grasslands and forests for oxygen production**.
   Get a bucket of water, two pie pans, and a small kitchen sponge. Ask an adult to help you cut a piece of wood the same size as the sponge. Soak the sponge and the block of wood in the bucket of water for awhile. Take them out of the water and put each in a pie pan. Which holds more water? Why?

   Green plants give off oxygen that people and other animals need to breathe. Trees and forests get credit for giving off a lot of oxygen, but grasslands are like sponges, and forests are like blocks of wood. Which do you think gives off the most oxygen? Why?

3. Plant the right grasses.

Not all grasses grow equally well in all places. Visit your local lawn and garden shop. Buy a small amount of seeds for Kentucky bluegrass, tall fescue, and red rye. Make three separate plots, and plant a small amount of each grass type in each plot. Water one plot a little each day, water another plot every other day, and water the third plot once a week. What happens to the different kinds of grasses with the different amounts of water? Which grass should be grown where a lot of rain falls? Which should be grown where only a little rain falls?

Things You Can Do to Help

1. **Get more information**. Ask your teacher to invite guest speakers to talk to your class about grasslands. Visit your town library. Find the nature section and read the books on prairies and grasslands. Ask local nature clubs to donate books about the grasslands to the library.

2. **Find the grasslands near your home.** Call or write your state wildlife, parks, or natural resources department and ask for information about local grasslands. Ask for maps that show where the grasslands are and how to get there. Ask if any local grassland has a visitor center, guided tours, or an outdoor classroom. Plan a field trip to visit that grassland with your class or family.

3. **Spread the word.** Help others learn about how important grasslands are. Plan a Prairie Celebration Day at your school. Organize activities that show your friends and classmates how much has already been lost from the grasslands and how much needs to be protected.

Places to Write for More Information

No one large organization has information about all the grasslands around the world or even just in the United States. However, many small, local groups work with grassland issues. The Nature Conservancy can help you find and get in touch with grassland groups near where you live. When you write them, be sure to tell them exactly what you want to know, and include an envelope with a stamp and your name and address so they can write back to you.

The Nature Conservancy
1815 North Lynn
Arlington, Virginia
22209

National Grasslands
  Visitor Center
708 Main Street
Wall, South Dakota
57790

Society for the Protection
  of the Environment
P.O. Box 370
Stellenbosch 7600
South Africa

More Books to Read

The Prairie World, by David Costello (Thomas Y. Crowell Co.)
Grasslands, edited by Lauren Brown (Alfred Knopf)
Natural Kansas, edited by Joseph T. Collins (University of Kansas Press)

Glossary

annual — a plant that lives for only one growing season.

bison — a very large grazing animal of North America, often called a "buffalo."

browse — to eat mostly woody plants.

estivate — to go into a deep sleep to survive dry periods.

forbs — plants that are not grasses and have large or wide leaves but no wood.

fossorial — living in the ground by burrowing in the soil.

graze — to eat grasses and forbs.

herbivore — any animal that eats plants.

irrigate — to add extra water to crops.

lek — a small area where certain kinds of birds gather for mating.

migrate — to move back and forth between places and between seasons.

perennial — a plant that lives more than two growing seasons.

plain — a flat, or mostly flat, area of land.

prairie — an area where mostly grasses grow, usually on a plain.

precipitation — water that falls to the ground from clouds, such as rain, sleet, hail, and snow.

rhizome — a plant stem that grows underground; not the same as a root.

skylark — to fly up in the air and sing while fluttering back to the ground.

sodbusting — plowing grassland soil that has never been plowed.

tiller — a small grass plant that grows from the side of a larger grass plant.

Index